ANTHOLOGY OF POETRY
BY
YOUNG AMERICANS®

2002 EDITION
VOLUME CC

Published by Anthology of Poetry, Inc.

©*Anthology of Poetry by Young Americans*®
2002 Edition
Volume CC

All Rights Reserved©

Printed in the United States of America

To submit poems
for consideration in the year 2003 edition of the
Anthology of Poetry by Young Americans®,
send to: poetry@asheboro.com or

      Anthology of Poetry, Inc.
      PO Box 698
      Asheboro, NC 27204-0698

Authors responsible
for originality of poems submitted.

The Anthology of Poetry, Inc.
307 East Salisbury • P.O. Box 698
Asheboro, NC   27204-0698

Paperback ISBN: 1-883931-33-9
Hardback ISBN: 1-883931-32-0

Anthology of Poetry by Young Americans®
is a registered trademark of
Anthology of Poetry, Inc.

Our scattered flocks at play in the fields on that crystal-blue morning.

It has been a year where we've seen our rivers of faith run momentarily backward, heard our symphonic voice of unity splinter into a cacophony of cries, and felt our hearts pull tight with the erratic beat of panic. It has been the year when we found our collective soul, and reconstituted our American fiber.

In the thirteen years since the first Anthology of Poetry by Young Americans® was published, no single school year has meant so much to the parents, children, and dedicated teachers. This has been a year where we've seen the hearts of our young fill with hope and worry, uncertainty and faith, with love and anger. In the eyes of our children we've seen the look of need, the expression of love, and the want of new words. As time stood still and the force of survival demanded their strength, they grew before our very eyes. We held them close and we wiped their tears. To us, they gave back hope.

Let us now listen. It is time for the youth of this great country to share with us their thoughts, to share with us their vision, to share with us their promise of an American future.

Gather now our scattered flocks at play in the fields on this crystal-blue morning…

Our growing family at the Anthology of Poetry, Inc. sends our love, sympathies, and hope to the thousands of families forever changed on the morning of September 11, 2001.

The Editors

AMERICA STANDS TALL

America is our country, with people standing tall,
Even if cruel people caused us a great fall.
We all say: Hooray for the red, white, and blue!
We show American pride, and help each other too.

This tragedy has caused us all so many tears,
It has filled us with so many fears.
But this horrendous act has pulled us together,
And we Americans will stay that way forever.

We all express our greatest sorrows,
Hoping it will be better tomorrow.
For tomorrow is another day,
And maybe, just maybe, it will go our way.

Some people showed us an act of hate,
But our country is truly great.
The things we Americans are so proud of,
Is freedom, liberty, happiness, and love.

GOD BLESS AMERICA!

Akari Anderson

I was expected to be perfect.
I learned math.
I've held a chick and a chicken.
I've heard secrets from my older cousin.
I lost money.
I've had some ice cream.
I tell you sincerely I love math.
I saw a chicken and chicks.
I once screamed at my little sister.
Twice I changed her diapers.
I have a baby sister.
I bought candy and Slurpies.
I've been scared of dark.
I have stories of my childhood.
The smell of roses reminds me of my grandma.
I have shopped at Kmart.

I'm Russian!

Mark Shitefanio
Age: 10

Ned was a cow.
Everyone knew how to take a bow.
When he was in a play,

You could hear him say,
Oh, check it out baby,
Right here is where kids can get crazy.

Eric Baccellieri
Age: 8

UP IN THE AIR

How I love to go up off the ground,
feeling my feet touch the sky.
I think that every person around
should experience the joy to fly.
I like to feel my toes off the floor,
and my limbs flowing freely about.
I would like to sail right out the door,
to a land with no fear or doubt.
Up in the air it's revealed to me,
and that is where I want to be.

Alexis A. Shusterman
Age: 10

WALLS

The walls are a beaut,
The walls are cute,
Walls with dolls
And waterfalls,
Filled with joy
And as fun as a toy.
The children watch out
For the pictures jump
And turn into real living things.

Andrea Rano
Age: 8

APRIL

April
Rainy sunny
My little brother's birthday, dog
Great and very very exciting
Rainy

Adam Millner
Age: 9

NEVER GIVE UP

When you fall down, get right back up.
When you scrape your knee or fall in the dirt,
Get right back up.
When you try and try, just try some more.
Never give up!

Sa - Leah Rose Noland
Age: 9

I'M THE ONE WHO

I'm the one who sees Sam
lying in the sand-filled hospital bed.
The one who sees the dimly lighted room of the ICU.
The one who sees the doctor
telling Mom and Dad what's wrong.

I'm the one who hears the "beep"
of the heart monitor.
The one who hears the nurses
talking about their patients.
The one who hears the visitors talking quietly
amongst themselves in the waiting room.

I'm the one who believes Sam will survive.
The one who believes I will be away from hospitals
for the rest of my life.

I'm the one who wants my brother
to be away from this place.
The one who wants Sam out of his wheelchair.
And most of all I'm the one who wants Sam
to never be stared at again.

Nathan Lightner
Age: 11

I'M THE ONE WHO

I'm the one who sees brown and red leaves
blowing across the street,
the dark black cloudy sky
heading towards my house,
the rain falling sideways
making puddles on the sidewalk.

I'm the one who hears soft music
coming from the speakers,
the birds scraping their claws on the gutter
as they search for food,
and dinner being served as night falls over the city.

I'm the one who smells the steak
my dad barbecues for dinner,
the fresh rain coming off my dog's coat
as she comes in from playing outside,
and the aroma of my mom's caramel cake
as she prepares it for my birthday.

I'm the one who tastes my mom's
freshly baked cookies as they melt in my mouth,
the popcorn so buttery and salty
it makes my mouth water,
and McDonald's French fries
that are greasy and soft.

I'm the one who feels the basketball grips
as I dribble down the court to make a basket,
the sticky rice as it clings to my fingers
so I can't get it off,
the computer keys as I type in my password
to my favorite game.

I'm the one who wants the pollution
to stop filtering over our state,
once again to see my old cat, Tom Christmas,
who died at my aunt's farm,
people to stop littering
and make our world a better place.

I'm the one who believes if we work together
we will accomplish our goals,
you should always believe in yourself,
if you get angry toward your goals
you will hardly ever achieve them!

Allison Gano
Age: 11

MARK'S HOUSE

I see Mark's house in the apartments
in front of the woods.
I smell the nice fresh smell of the woods.
I go in the woods and feel the tall plants
rubbing against my body.
I hear the birds singing away
and talking to each other.
The smell and sound relaxes me.
Finally the day is over and I go in his house.
We stay up a long time playing video games.
I fall asleep very easy.
His back door to his balcony is open
and I can smell and hear the woods.
I fall asleep.
I wake up, I can't even taste the waffles I am eating.
It feels like I'm tasting the woods,
but I can't taste the waffles.
I'm daydreaming.
When I get home I can still smell the woods.
I'm going there before I know it.
I will go again, I know I know know...

Sam Knight
Age: 10

OCTOBER NIGHTS

I get into my frigid bed at night.
The brisk sheets cover my body.
I hear the rain outside
as it hits the gutter with a large splash.
The icy wind blows through the window
as it sends shivers down my spine.
I get up to shut my window.
I can feel the hard wooden floor
as I sneak closer and closer.
I climb back into my bed.
It soon grows quiet and all I can hear
is the chirp of the crickets
and the rushing of the cars going by.
My eyelids get heavy as I drift off to sleep.
I know October nights.

Kalie Papasadero
Age: 10

A DAY AT THE PARK

My brother and I went to the park.
I see the trees with their brilliant green leaves
    swaying in the wind.
I hear the birds singing in the trees.
I feel the cold windy fresh air.
I hear the crunch of the leaves
    under my dirty blue tennis shoes.
I can smell the smoky air of a barbecue.

Emily R. Hudson
Age: 10

THE UNITED PART OF AMERICA

Yesterday when I walked the street,
I saw the poverty,
people holding out signs that say
they have nothing to eat.
But now I see that things can be worse
than you think possible.

I have known, forever, that there were
horrible things happening in the world.
I knew that seven out of ten deaths
could be prevented,
I just never really thought about it much.

But here I am, mourning the deaths
of five thousands of people who I knew.
I did not used to know them, but I do now know
that they each were part of me.
Part of the United States of America.

When I was little, I used to think that America
was invincible, impossible to destroy.
Now I realize how right I was, except one little thing:

The military is not why we are invincible,
but the spirit of the people,
our willing to help each other.

God Bless America.

Gwen Kaplin

GRANDPARENTS

My grandparents are nice.
It's 3:00 it's time to get ice cream.
It tastes like cream, minty, doughy
when it goes down your throat.
It's the nicest day.
We have waffles, mm, I love Grandma's
waffles are syrupy-crunchy.
My grandma and grandpa are nice to me
they should rule the world.
What I like about my grandma
is her cards off the computers.
What I like about my grandpa
is that he is the funniest man.
What else I like about Grandma
is when we go on the beach for a walk with Holly.
I like to go on the beach on July 4th
because I like to blast off fireworks.

Ben Oswald
Age: 10

GRANDPARENTS

My grandparents are nice
just like an angel
flying in the sky,
blue and wide,
deep and strong,
I love them
because they're just like my parents,
and that's why
that's why
I love my grandparents
so much,
that you would
believe it's true,
I do love them so much,
because they help me
when I need help,
and they're always there for me
because they care for me,
I love them
even though sometimes
they're mean to me
but I still care about them
because they are my guardians.

Jenae Johnson - Eerkes
Age: 10

WHAT YOU WOULD FIND IN A COMPOST PILE

A rotten orange,
A banana peel,
A skeleton of an electric eel,
Cream cheese with a moldy green slime,
Eggshell, all white and prime,
Moldy bread and burnt toast,
Corn on the cob eaten delightfully (most),
These are the things you'll find in a compost pile,
(Not the things that would make you smile),
Oh yes, that's what you find in a compost pile,
(Each with a smell rather vile),
My friends,
THAT'S WHAT YOU FIND IN A COMPOST PILE!

Emma Franz
Age: 8

MY HOME

My home so sweet.
Our happy treat.
We're happy when we're there together.
No matter what kind of weather.
We have good times and like to play.
We're happy together every day.

Alyssa Frangipani
Age: 9

MY FAMILY ON THE BOAT

We go on the boat,
Riding through the sparkling water
it looks like diamonds from the flaming hot sun.
I hear the loud music against my ears from the radio.
I feel the rough wakes of the other boats passing by.
I smell the clean fresh air that surrounds me,
the boat and the river.
I hear my dad's YAAHOO!!!
As he jumps in the water from the bow.
I feel shivering cold now that the sun is down,
with my black sandals and my white T-shirt.

Sean Cochran
Age: 10

KITTIES, KITTIES

My kitty's name is Sara,
She's very frisky and fair.

I always keep the lookout
Because she is very rare.

She's just like a regular cat,
But just a little meaner.

Kelsey McGinnis
Age: 8

ANOTHER'S EYES

Look into the eyes of a stranger
And tell me what you see
Hurt or hope?
Fear or surprise?
Imagine what you look like
Through another's eyes.
Tell me what you think of
When you look in the mirror.
Do you cringe to see your face
Or just wave it aside?
Imagine what someone else sees.
Have you ever tried?
Some would have you
Walk a mile in a stranger's shoes.
But all I say,
Is just for a moment
Look inside.
And peer at yourself,
Through another's eyes.

Cassandra Ellwood
Age: 13

BLUEBIRD'S SPINNING

Memories are a spindle
a spindle in your mind.
The thread a long list
of memories
Around and around it whirls
where it stops nobody knows.
A teardrop
a single memory of one.
It plots a course
down your cheek
No stopping it; No courage
to wipe it away.
The spindle whirls again.
Lightning, a branch across the sky
The shock;
the thrill.
Excitement jolts through you;
lights up the sky,
amazed by lightning's energy.
The spindle and thread move again.
Laughter echoes;
echoes off the walls
of your mind.
Reaches every corner.
Laughter of friends
and yours,
parties, truth-or-dare, secrets
crushes, heartbreaks
Friends and the best of the best: Laughter.

The spindle moves again
to continue the thread,
the string,
the yarn,
of your memories.

Erin Britt
Age: 13

I WONDER IF...

I wonder if I had no rooms, no walls, no halls,
   And not even a bed.
Then I would have no clothes, no gloves, no shoes,
   And nothing to cover my head.

I wonder if I had no food, no water, no corn,
   And not even bread.
I want to be alive,
   But I might be dead.

I wonder if I had no furniture, no table, no couch,
   And not even a chair.
Then my whole house would be bare.

I wonder if I had no family, no brother, no sister,
   And not even a friend.
I can't talk about it,
   So, I guess it's the end.

Melissa Wallis
Age: 8

AMERICA, AMERICA

America, America,
What does it mean to me?
America, America,
A land of freedom and opportunity.

But what factors
Make this country great?
Its wonderful citizens
From each and every state.

The United States is quite diverse,
But it doesn't discriminate
Against its many different peoples.
That's what makes it great.

America is beautiful.
America is grand.
Nowhere near or far
Can beat this great land.

Of all the countries,
I don't hesitate to say
I'm glad to call my home
The one and only U. S. A.!

Jonathan A. Walsh

PATRIOTIC

We all looked up shocked by what had happened,
We were mad,
We were sad.

Now when you look at the sky,
You expect to see two tall Towers,
But you don't have to look down,
Because it all lies right in front of you.

But we stick together through,
Thick and thin,
We all help each other.

I guess in a way
It's like the great fire in Chicago.

So if we stick together
No more lives will be ruined,
With what had happened
Many lives already have been ruined,
Children without parents,
Brothers without sisters,
Sisters without brothers,
Husbands without wives
Or wives without husbands
And friends without friends.

That is how our lives have changed.

GOD BLESS AMERICA

Shervin D. Sima

F earless!
I mportant people,
R eady to help all.
E mergency!
M any of them
E nthusiastic!
N ational heroes!

Brian Lunsford

SEPTEMBER 11TH TRAGEDY

So many faces we have lost
for what was the cause.
It took our nation by surprise,
worried feelings deep inside.
With Jesus by our side, we took pride.
The damage they have caused
I wish they would of not.
Where do we go from here?
First, we go in prayer.
Then we pray some more
from sea to shining sea.

Brittney Rose de Alicante

RED, WHITE, BLUE

Red, white, blue,
My country's colors.
People live in unity
And don't loathe each other.

We live together.
We talk together.

After the happening,
Sorrow filled our hearts,
But, we still stand united.
We opened our hearts and minds,
As we took New York in,
Trying to ease great pain.
We pretend nothing happened,
But, we still know it did.

We live together,
We talk together,
We walk together.
Red, white, blue,
My family's colors.

Morgan R. Jemerson

THANKSGIVING

Thank You
for all my hands can hold --
my blanket that my mom made me
and my teddy bear, Sophie,
that sits on my bed.

Thank You
for all my eyes can see --
family and friends.

Thank You
for all my ears can hear --
my cats purring on my lap
and my dad whistling.

Maya Berns - Janousek
Age: 7

WHAT A MOTHER IS LIKE

M akes you dinner.
O n her schedule.
T eaches you things.
H elps you.
E verybody loves her.
R eally works hard.

Claire Calhoun
Age: 8

THANKSGIVING

Thank You
for all my hands can hold --
the M&M's that my grandpa gives me
and my cat J.B.

Thank You
for all my eyes can see --
kids W.B. 32 on TV
and my cat, J.B., that is nice.

Thank You
for all my ears can hear --
rap music on 95.5
and movies that have funny sounds.

Jamison Vogt
Age: 7

MY HORSE

I see Turbo walk on the grass
   and gallop free around the stable
I hear him chew his hay and grain --
   happy to be himself
I feel his hair as I brush him
I can smell the dust when Turbo runs wild and free --
   glad to be a horse
I can taste some hay in my mouth
   from giving Turbo hay

Allison Stofiel
Age: 10

I'M THE ONE WHO...

I'm the one who sees the house across the street,
the American flags on cars and the different color
leaves falling off the autumn trees.

I'm the one who smells flowers
in the summer breeze,
dough baking into delicious cookies
and coffee brewing in the morning.

I'm the one who hears bashing and banging of pans
when I'm asleep, rain on the roof,
and the loud RAP songs on the radio.

I'm the one who tastes the chewy gum in my mouth,
syrupy hot waffles and cold fruity yogurt
before school.

I'm the one who touches cold, slimy watermelon
on a hot summer day, a warm woolly blanket
around me on a cold winter night
and the soft silky fur of a purring kitten.

I'm the one who wants everyone
to be treated equally in the world,
to catch Osama bin Laden
and who wants the world to be a better place.

I'm the one who fears that new terrorists
will come back, afraid because my grandpas are sick
and afraid about going to a new middle school.

I'm the one who believes that everybody is equal,
I believe in God
and I believe the world will be peaceful again.

Carly Christie

THE BIG SPIDER

One day when I was in my room,
Just listening to some music,
I saw a spider as big as me creep onto my knee.
It said, "Say, would you like to play?"
I screamed and ran.
I ran the wrong way.
He said, "Hey, weren't we going to play?"

Elizabeth Lundberg

THANKSGIVING

Thank You
for all my hands can hold --
my mom's gold cross
and my birthstone ring.

Thank You
for all my eyes can see --
my two cats
and my two dogs.

Thank You
for all my ears can hear --
birds chirping
and the loud sounds of snowmobiles.

Ashley Baker
Age: 7

SOCCER

Up the field
Down the field
Around the field
Across the field
Kick
Kick
Kick
Score!!!

Olivia Wallace

I'M HUNGRY

I'm hungry I say I'm hungry
I need some food to eat
I'll die if I don't
I'm hungry give me give me I need to eat

Molly Rashoff
Age: 10

THANKSGIVING

Thank You
for all my hands can hold --
my furry stuffed animal
named Rufus and my pink
teddy bear blanket.

Thank You
for all my eyes can see --
my mom and dad
and my dog and my brother Andrew.

Thank You
for all my ears can hear --
dogs barking loudly
and birds chirping.

Sarah Sanderson
Age: 7

THE TEARS OF THE HOLOCAUST

So small and young they were
by being of a different religion they were...
excluded, humiliated, moved and full of grief
discrimination was everywhere!
The war brought out the worst of people.
Being on trains with people side to side
was torture.
Heading for nothing more than death
Camps were filled with mournful faces
Meaningful tears spoke the words
they could not say.
For the people and children
who had not been taken to a camp
all they could do was hide and hope they would
not be found.
Nazis constantly revealing the hiding faces
that they found.
Hearts filled with so much pain
that they could not speak the feeling they had.
Year after year the torture continued.
So many tears it could fill
a lake, river, even an ocean.
1945 the time had finally came.
Most of the ethnic jokes had come to a stop.
Camps were closed and people were free.
New lives were beginning.
This time tears were of joy
and could be spoken of happy words.
Children back in school, parents and adults in work.

But they had something left of the horrible times
the memories remained in those who were alive
their heads had a memory
which was too tragic to remember.
The cries, voices and screams for help
lay in their heads waiting to be freed.
Education was being passed out to all the children
Learning was their first priority.
People grew and children exceeded.
Continued through life.
But to all of the people who had memories
they can only hope.
Hope something like this will never happen again.
The dreams people have
and so little time to make them all come true!

Amy Elizabeth Galloway
Age: 13

I WISH I HAD A CAT

I wish I had this
I wish I had that
I have a doll
I have a dog
I even have a toy frog
But most of all
I wish I had a cat!!!

Kathleen Lance
Age: 8

THANKSGIVING

Thank You
for all my hands can hold --
my three half dollars
and my two soccer trophies.

Thank You
for all my eyes can see --
my cat jumping on my bed
and my mom tucking me in my bed.

Thank You
for all my ears can hear --
my cat purring in my ear
and my mom talking to my friend's mom.

Jake E. Souza
Age: 7

ALWAYS WITH US IS OUR GOD

A lways with us is our God
M ay He never leave us
E very day, our God is with us
R emember His forgiveness and love for us
I n our hearts our God lives
C an we be kind like He was
A wesome is our God

Jon D'Ambrosia
Age: 8

SAYING GOOD-BYE

I'm just a little kid,
But I am growing fast,
You'll miss me when I go,
You'll wish it was the past.

You do not realize now,
That every second means,
That you have one less second,
To spend with both your teens.

Your love can't be described,
It's too strong to put in words,
You'll miss your little angels,
When they fly away like birds.

You do not get the concept,
Of letting go your prize,
But I can tell you this,
You must undo your ties.

Robyn Wolochow

WHEN THE KITE WENT UP

I was sitting on my favorite rocking chair
one blustery night, when I heard a knock at the door.
I opened it. It was Benjamin Franklin,
the most famous man in town.
"Good evening Mr. Franklin," I said,
"What are you doing on such a blustery night?"
"I'm doing an experiment my boy,
well I'm trying to do an experiment."
I wondered why he would ever be at my house,
until he said,
"Do you have a nice medium sized kite my boy?"
Now I know why he came to my house,
I was the kite maker in the town.
I made kites for all the little children in the village.
So I rushed down to my workshop
and got the best medium sized kite I had.
I asked what his experiment was.
"I'm going to send a metal key up into the clouds
to see if it will attract the lightning!," he replied.
"Now I'm off, and thank you," he said.

I ran to the window to see what would happen.
He tied a key to the string of the kite.
The kite went up. A lightning bolt struck,
missing the kite, then another.
Another one struck, hitting the key!
The key sparkled in the darkness.
Mr. Franklin fell to the ground.
I ran to get my coat on
so I could go outside and help him.
Then I heard another knock at the door.
It was Mr. Franklin.
Oh, thank goodness he was all right, I thought.
But he was covered in a black substance.
He smelled terrible, and the kite was in shambles.
All that was left of it
was the wooden border and a bit of cloth.
He handed me the remains of the kite, thanked me
and ran off yelling, "I've got it!"
He woke up the whole town.

Brendan Robinson

There was a young man of Kabul,
Who spun yarn for his rugs on a spool.
His carpets were magic,
But his story is tragic.
He leaned backwards and fell off his stool.

James Dylan Page
Age: 12

SPRING

Pink petals cover the ground
Like corpses
The flowers are gone from the trees,
Save a few stubborn survivors
    -- late bloomers
Spring is gone and what remains
Is the thick scent of cherry in the air
I breathe it deep into my lungs
And it starts to decay there
   -- my breath grows shorter
   -- my skin peels off like scales,
    it is tougher than it seems
How strange it is to lose my fingerprints
To see them lying useless on their own
How strange it is to watch
These silent flowers bloom
   Tainting this clean water with the color of passion
   And the swollen ripe cherries of summer.

Sarah Mori Hunter
Age: 17

Fall
bright, fiery
falling, floating, spinning
Leaves are falling everywhere.
Colorful

Meredith Wood
Age: 11

THANKSGIVING

Thank You
for all my hands can hold --
my ring that has my birthstone in it
and my best friend
necklace that has a teddy bear on it.

Thank You
for all my eyes can see --
all the colors in the world
and my friends when they smile.

Thank You
for all my ears can hear --
my mom when she hums at work
and my dad when he tells me a funny
and happy story.

Alicia Mendiola
Age: 7

SWIMMING AND DIVING

Swimming is wet
Gliding through the water, like a fish
Diving
Flying through the air.
Your arms cut through the water
No splash
Arms, legs, all work together
To make you dive and swim.

Leslie Hawkins
Age: 11

I AM

Call me Brandon.
I like rats.
I want an amusement park in my backyard.

I yell at my sister.
I laugh a lot.

I always talk.
I never have been to Mexico.

I wonder if I'm going to get a swimming pool?
I wish I had a car.

I am crazy.

Brandon Seliner
Age: 11

WIND

Wind
fierce, powerful
howling, crying, moving
It blows you down.
Mean

Jordan Rowland
Age: 11

I AM

Call me a pianist.

I like going to Hawaii every year.
I want a snake for a pet.

I yell when I have a lot of energy.
I laugh and laugh and can't stop laughing.

I always liked the color blue.
I never yell at my brother even when I want to.

I wonder what the world will be like in the 3,000's.
I wish I could go to every state in the U. S.

I am Courtney Anne Humphrey.

Courtney Anne Humphrey
Age: 11

Fall
cold, windy
running, splashing, pouring
Wind blows golden leaves.
Windy pleasure

Kial A. Collins
Age: 11

THANKSGIVING

Thank You
for all my hands can hold --
my silver guardian angel necklace
that I love and my special bonnet
that my grandma gave to me.

Thank You
for all my eyes can see --
the sun shining so bright
and the colors around me.

Thank You
for all my ears can hear --
my doll that sings "Jesus Loves Me"
and my mom humming at night
before I fall asleep.

Addylee Torian
Age: 8

AMERICA

America is strong.
America will be here forever.
America is unbeatable.
America will not fall.
We can be shocked.
But we will not fall.

Andrew Cobb
Age: 11

WHAT ART IS

Art is expression.
Art is beauty.
Art is magic.
Art is freedom.
Art is refinement.
Art is wildness.
Art is nature.
Art is the human race.
Art is a dream.
Art is order.
Art is a spirit.
Art is many things;
Yet, art is undefineable.

Madeleine Johnson
Age: 11

Fall
windy, nippy
gusting, jumping, scattering
Leaves are coming down.
Autumn

Derek Voreis
Age: 11

THANKSGIVING

Thank You
for all my hands can hold --
my teddy bear named Maggie Anne
and an apple that is red and tastes good
in my mouth.

Thank You
for all my eyes can see --
my mom and my dad
and my family.

Thank You
for all my ears can hear --
when I go to the beach I can hear
a song in the waves
and my birds chirping.

Laura Hastings
Age: 7

WIND

wind swoops
  down
    down
      like a hawk searching every nook and cranny
    strong as steel
the wind laughs at every door whistling and howling
      like little night creatures
    always mysterious as an owl at night
    as nothingness
      but always there

Gwynneth Johnson
Age: 12

MY PARENTS...

My parents love me!
My parents are kind.
My parents are caring
and love me head to toes.
My parents are giving.
My parents receive.
My parents are healthy
and good to me.
My parents help me
with things like homework.
My parents love me!

Chelsea Barthelemy
Age: 11

41

BASEBALL

The ball leaves the pitcher's hand,
And then the batter swings,
While the stands are teasing,
I am feeling queasy,
"Boy those nachos were greasy."
While Mom is eating some too,
And Grandpa is having a little snooze,
That is the life at the park,
Where baseball is not new.

Mason Rippey
Age: 12

FOOTBALL

Football is the most exciting sport.
You can crash, you can bash;
You might get hurt.
But that's OK it's too fun to care.
You can tackle, run, jump.
You may not win but do not fret
Get up and play again.
You can score a touchdown;
Or make them fumble,
And even get a safety!
Have you played football?

Jake Geiszler
Age: 12

SALMON

eggs.
their
lay
to
just
energy
life and
up all
Giving
waterfall.
of the big
at the top
claws
Bear's
Grizzly
the
through
Slipping
in bait.
lathered
all
hooks
fisher's
past the
Swimming
the stream.
swim up
slowly
Salmon

Kathryn A. Vander Weele
Age: 12

THANKSGIVING

Thank You
for all my hands can hold --
my books I like to read
and my mom's hand
that I like to hold.

Thank You
for all my eyes can see --
my friends that I love
and my family that I love.

Thank You
for all my ears can hear --
my family talking to me
and me talking to my family.

B. J. Shapiro - Albert
Age: 7

Wanders the forest,
Wanders the streets,
Wanders the desert looking for men.

Not God

Healthy and young,
All are victims,
To the cause of all things that have died.

Not time

Some are afraid,
Some are not scared,
Some are awaiting their meeting with God

Black

You will depart,
You aren't too young,
Your meeting with God will be perfect and gold.

DEATH

Garrett Lee
Age: 11

THE SEASONS

A shower of rain,
Mud on the ground,
A flower has been found,
It's spring.

A blast of heat,
A blinding light,
Soon the birds will take flight,
It's summer.

A soft whisper,
A gentle breeze,
Leaves are falling from the trees,
It's fall.

A gust of wind,
A rush of snow,
Soon flowers will grow,
It's winter.

It's the end of winter,
It's the end of a whole new year,
Listen closely with your ear,
It's the new year!

Caroline Kokubun
Age: 11

BUILDING COMMUNITY

Busy people working so hard,
Wearing their "busy" masks.
They lose the chance to find pure joy
By skipping simple tasks.
Like giving to the needy,
The helpless and the poor.
Or cleaning up a park
So it is clean as was before.
Or giving to small children,
Who do not have a toy.
Or visiting the elderly
Who need a little joy.
For giving love to those around
Brings joy into your heart.
The tasks you do and love you give
Show that you'll do your part.
For when you love another,
You build community.
You help to shape what this world
Will one day, with your help, be.

Allison Krause
Age: 11

IMAGINATION

The strength of each song,
The right of every wrong,
The soul of every heart,
And for every journey the start.

Is imagination.

Across the fields of creation,
And the feelings and sensations,
Inside all jubilation,
Yields an endless nation

Of imagination.

The heart behind all hope,
The curl of every smoke,
The wind behind each dove,
The force of fruited love,

Is imagination.

The light of every shade,
The dew on each grass blade,
The choking endless dark,
The coarseness of aged bark,

Is imagination.

Imagination, imagination.
Since the beginning of creation,
Creating blessed salvation,
It is love's foundation

Truthful,
Youthful,
Curing
Enduring,

Imagination.

Logan Johnston
Age: 13

THANKSGIVING

Thank You
for all my hands can hold --
my bear that my grandmother gave me
before she died and a butterfly.
I like it when the butterfly kisses me.

Thank You
for all my eyes can see --
my cat Smoky
that my brother shares with me
and a bird soaring over my head.

Thank You
for all my ears can hear --
the whales that sing in my ears
and crickets chirping in my ears.

Nathan Baxter - MacDonald
Age: 7

DRAMA

D evoting your time to practice and plays
R eciting the script by memory onstage
A cting out your character
M iming is part of drama too
A ctors and actresses have fun doing what they do.

Adrianna Wagner
Age: 11

I wake up in the morning.
  Why, because I'm told to.
I shower and eat breakfast.
  Why, because I'm told to.
I go to school in the morning.
  Why, because I'm told to.
I go to all my classes.
  Why, because I'm told to.
After school I go to football practice.
  Why, because I'm told to.
I go home and do my homework.
  Why, because I'm told to.
I eat dinner and go to bed.
  Why, because I'm told to.
I live my life day in and day out.
  Why... because I'm told to.

David Williams
Age: 14

PARROTS

P layful and cute
A lways very funny
R ough to their toys
R eally loud at certain times
O n shoulders are where they like to be
T hey come in different colors
S ilent and graceful

Emily McLaughlin
Age: 10

THE NEWSPAPER

My dad's in love with the newspaper
He reads it every day.
The newspaper was his first love
Before my mommy Jaye.

My dad's in love with the newspaper
He can't seem to stop reading it.
The only thing that can stop him
Is to watch the news on TV.
How can this be?
Doesn't he get enough of this stuff?

My dad's in love with the newspaper
The newspaper, the newspaper
He reads it every day.

Danika Raye Douglas
Age: 7

JOSHUA E. CLAPPER

I am intelligent and loving.
I wonder what good or bad things may happen.
I hear music.
I see mysterious illusions in the dark.
I want to collect something from every continent.
I am intelligent and loving.

I pretend I am a great leader.
I feel and know I am loved.
I need to have a hug from someone every day.
I worry about my family and pets.
I cry when I think of memories.
I am intelligent and loving.

I understand that you don't always get what you want.
I say I am important.
I dream freely.
I try to be a good role model.
I hope to be a good influence to people.
I am intelligent and loving.

Josh Clapper
Age: 11

JENNIFER MCCRAE

I am creative and loving,
I wonder if my grandma can take me to Denmark,
I hear singing,
I see Whiskey,
I want to be a teacher,
I am creative and loving.

I pretend I am a bird,
I feel like the youngest,
I need my dog Whiskey,
I worry about my cat Jasper,
I cry when I hear my best friend's name,
I am creative and loving.

I understand that nobody's perfect,
I say anyone is special if they think they are,
I dream that my bruise on my head will be better,
I try to be a good sister,
I hope to be with my brother and sister forever,
I am creative and loving.

Jennifer McCrae
Age: 10

KENNY L. REECK

I am smart and intelligent.
I wonder about what it'll be like to go to junior high.
I hear loud music.
I see oceans.
I want to be a sports superstar.
I am smart and intelligent.

I pretend to play baseball in the major league.
I feel like a snowboarder.
I need nutrients.
I worry about my rabbit.
I cry when I get hit by a baseball.
I am smart and intelligent.

I understand geography and math.
I say I don't like school.
I dream about no homework.
I try to think of the weekend.
I hope to be good at lots of stuff.
I am smart and intelligent.

Kenny Reeck
Age: 10

I AM DEVON

I am funny and energetic
I wonder when I can go off my bike jump
I hear talking at night
I see a red mountain bike with shocks
I want a brand-new mountain bike with shocks
I am funny and energetic

I pretend that I have a semi
I feel mad when people touch my stuff without asking
I need my mom when I'm sad
I worry when my mom goes to the hospital
I cry when I get hurt bad
I am funny and energetic

I understand when I cannot go with my dad in the semi
I say, "Free ice cream for everyone!"
I dream I have a python
I try to jump my bike high
I hope I get to play the cello
I am funny and energetic

Devon Molendyk
Age: 10

KITTY CAT

K ittens are little and playful,
I rresistible when I look at them,
T ruly and beautifully hearted,
T otal peace is filled inside of them.
Y ou can love them like a baby.

C uddly and cute, filled with joy,
A ttitude is always counted with love,
T ogether we are angels from above,
S weet and full of love, until the day they die...

Katrina Altona
Age: 11

KIDS

As I look around on this day,
I see a people laugh and be gay.
To run, to sit, to dance around
in this free world our forefathers found.
The problems in the world today
are forgotten by the children as they play.
They are a lesson for all the world
of the simplicity of the boy and girl.

Erin Franey
Age: 13

I spent two weeks at camp.
Camp Firwood is a rad place.
Swimming, boats, bikes, just for a few
And even some girls too!!!
Cool place, especially Scouch
Who, come to think of, was also our coach.
Marshmallows fire and hot dogs,
I remember towing those logs.
Late to bed, early to rise,
It's amazing nobody ever dies.
And really, come to think,
The food really doesn't stink.

Justyn Rath

BOG OF THE BUNNIES

Evil little bunnies, gnawing at my feet,
When I look down I see my bones
and feel a painful searing heat,
When I look up I see a hungry parakeet
hunting for my eyes,
I start to run on my stubs
while shielding from the biting flies.
Never again will I go back,
for any amount of money,
Never again will I go back to the bog,
the bog of the bunnies.

Zach Hoffman
Age: 12

ODE TO LOVE

Love is strong,
love is what we can choose to do.
We can love each other,
we can have anger for each other.
Our country can love everyone,
and we can feel like we hate each other.
We can smile,
we can frown,
but anyway we have love for everyone.
We have sorrow for each other,
we have excitement for each other.
We have love for other countries.
even though they may have hurt us in the past.
Our heart has enough love to support
every country.
Love is strong when you want it to be.
Love is for everybody
though they may not show it.
Once you have given love
to somebody you can take it back,
Just like no tag backs,
well...
no love backs.

Tesla Hovelman

ODE TO UNDERSTANDING

Why do some
Choose not to love,
Is it because they can't
I hope they just choose not to
But that's still sad,
But others choose to show love
And happiness
And make everything around them happy,
The ones who don't love
Will never be happy
And that is very sad
This nation will love and support
Every single person that needs us,
This is the nation
Of freedom
And love.

Michael Hidalgo

AIN'T NO LIFE

Well Tatyana, I'll tell you:
Life for me ain't been no walk in the park,
It's had rocks on the path,
Puddles full of mud
And great big holes, too.
Hard road
But all this time
I've been walking along
Makin' a bit of progress
Walkin' by tree after tree
Sometimes even stoppin' to let someone by.
But girl don't you take a seat on that cold bench
Don't you stop and stand around.
Don't stop movin'
Just 'cause you're tired
Or can't keep up.
And don't try and jump bushes,
Because you may get stuck
'Cause you see I'm still walkin'
And life ain't been no walk in the park.

Faith Willems
Age: 16

THE LAUGHING BROOK

Among the river of a laughing brook
whispered secretly to me.
I whispered back to it
a poem
bees and trees
and flowers blowing against the wind.
The laughing brook laughed at me,
and I laughed too.

Lily Jean Chen
Age: 9

MY BED

In my warm bed
Seeing my colorful blanket
The sounds of me moving around
Black the insides of my eyelids
Then Dreamland comes out to play
Smells like my warm, joyful home
After I had fun in my dream world
The morning comes.
I wake up
Then my mind says to my bed I will be back
My bed is lonely
But I will return.

Rion Brandt

FRIENDS

F riendly and caring.
R eady to be by your side.
I ntelligent and cool.
E asily can get in fights.
N ever usually happens.
D oesn't let you down.
S hares personal thoughts.

Hayley Moore
Age: 10

ODE TO NEW YORK

New York people walking by
    When a huge plane comes through the sky
Into a building people die
    The only question is why
Why this anger why this rage
    The change of history in the turn of a page
Fear is in everyone
    No idea, none
All the people very sore
    Soon enough it'll be war
Missiles flying everywhere
    Just because someone didn't care
About life, he's such a dork
    I send hope to the people in New York

Adam Daniel Adrian

DRAWING

D oing something with your imagination
R unning together to make a picture
A wonderful masterpiece
W aiting, just waiting to get the colors she needed
I n time to show people your
N eon colors that make it so bright so you can get a
G old medal for your hard work.

Karen Brignone
Age: 11

AMERICA

America the brave, America the strong,
    We still hold a mighty song.
We were broken but we will mend.
    Together we survive and will not end.
This country is great it has a hold.
    All of us will stand up straight and bold.
This country will survive its pain.
    Hold up our flag, we will sustain.
Of our nation all are proud
    We will proclaim it to aloud.
You the brave, you the strong,
    You help sing America's song.

Anne Wolfstone
Age: 12

9/11/01

We all woke up one morning
Everything was fine
Until we stopped a'snoring
There was no terrible crime

We turned on the morning news
And all our jaws dropped
At the horrifying things that people tend to do

None of us suspected
It was totally out of the blue
We didn't feel protected
And we didn't know what to do

First we started crying
At the frightful sight
As we saw people dying
We seemed to sit there until night

Then it was time to go to school
And see faces full of tears
Nothing seemed to be very cool
While I was crying with my peers

All the laughs were muffled
All the smiles were fake
Around each corner was a snuffle
And people burning at the stake

Everybody was proud
To be an American standing tall
We all were so loud
When we made that telephone call

And knew our friends and family,
W ere safe none the less
We were so overjoyed,
But there was an aching in our chests
We couldn't seem to forget the children
That had nothing left

Now we are still sad
But we now know
That the past is very bad
And underneath the snow

We should be thankful
For every little thing
People knocking at our door
For a bell they will ring

And with that bell, will come singing
From the young and the old
While that bell they are ringing
Standing out in the cold

To put a little sunshine
Into a sad heart
Because they miss that special mind
Now that they are apart

Their special person gone forever
They cry every night
For they are really gone forever
Never to return to sight

So love all that you know
You'll never know what could happen
It could be a normal day, when poof there they go

Mia Garrett
Age: 11

LIFE

The baby cries wild
As a whale sinks down
Life is a weird thing

Shay Byington
Age: 12

THE OLD MAN

He sits alone in a creaky rocking chair
The dust settles 'round him
He doesn't seem to care
With a big heart, and small hands
He lives lonely on these cold lands
Wife is gone
Children are grown
All three with families
But he is alone
The light in the attic burned out long ago
Because in that old attic, there's nothing to show
His dog at the fireplace
The cat at his feet
His only companions he is yet to meet
With lit pipe in his mouth
Smoke in a thin line
The small, little man
So gentle, so kind

Amanda Eggert
Age: 11

FRIENDS

F riends are always there.
R eally kind and helping.
I nventive and important to everyone.
E nergetic and creative.
N ever annoying and always fun.
D elightful to hang out with.
S chool and home is where you will find them.

Brianna Peterson
Age: 11

BIKE RACING

Bike racing is fun.
Bike racing is an adrenaline rush
that can only be had
when you're going as fast as you can,
and feel like you're flying.
Bike racing is going out
on a warm summer evening
and racing on the velodrome.
Bike racing is a race
against people, time, or even yourself.
Bike racing is life.

Rachelle Hobson
Age: 12

Summer
sunshine, hot
swimming, playing, gardening
baby animals, long days, short days, warm clothing
snow angels, snowmen, snowboarding
snow, cold
Winter

Melissa Lind
Age: 10

THANKSGIVING

Thank You
for all my hands can hold --
my gold necklace with a jewel on it
and my cat that purrs
when it's happy.

Thank You
for all my eyes can see --
my fish swimming in its container
and my teddy bear.

Thank You
for all my ears can hear --
music to my ears
from my Britney Spears tape
and birds chirping.

Ashton Babcock
Age: 7

MY MOUNTAIN IS MY LIFE

I have had too many tears,
I have had too many sorrows,
And when it all comes together,
It leads to depression
For all I have been through.

I keep on climbing my mountain.
I have slipped once,
Twice,
Three times, or more.
It is just like a ball game,
Three strikes, you're out.
Not for me.

People can say,
You won't make it,
Or you can't do that,
But, look at them,
At what they say,
Because they may not make it themselves.

My mom said paybacks come in weird ways
And, yes, they sure do.
So look at me now,
For I am close to the top of my mountain,
And I am not giving up.

Life's so hard at times,
But don't look down,
And it's closer than it seems.
You can do it if you put your mind to what you want
And don't give up,
And don't let others put you down.

There are a lot of things that can help you
And people who inspire you,
So, keep going
And you'll be at the top of your mountain soon.

Mariah Compean
Age: 10

DEAR LORD

Every morning I wake up and I feel you.
Every time I take a breath
you're in the morning breeze,
you're everywhere I look.
I know you see me
I know you help me in everything I do.
I can never stop thinking of you.
You're in my head, you're in my heart,
you're in my thoughts and dreams.
I pray to you Lord Jesus Christ,
make me happy make me intelligent,
because I know when you made me
you made me with love.

Megan Randi Scinocco
Age: 11

ANSWER

'   A ny days of my week I hear the
N ame I dare not
S peak the girl
W ith the cornhusk hair, my beloved and my despair
E very day I think of her. I
R eally must be quiet.

Travis Holst
Age: 11

THANKSGIVING

Thank You
for all my hands can hold --
my stuffed animal baby
and my blanket that my mom made for me.

Thank You
for all my eyes can see --
the beautiful nature in the woods
and the beautiful school
that I go to.

Thank You
for all my ears can hear --
the birds nice chirping
and the sea's waves splashing on the rocks.

Elizabeth Fennell
Age: 8

COLIN KENNEDY

I am nice and smart
I wonder about going to Scotland
I hear kids
I see black figures that zoom past my eyes
    but they are not there
I want a motorcycle
I am nice and smart

I pretend that I have a motorcycle
I feel that I have a motorcycle
I need a real motorcycle
I worry about my sister
I cry being mean to people
I am nice and smart

I understand that wrestling is not true
I say I believe that I will get a motorcycle
I dream that I have a motorcycle
I try to do the fiddle an effort
I hope that I will get a motorcycle
I am nice and smart

Colin Kennedy
Age: 11

TAYLOR SMITH

I am odd and funny.
I wonder what the world would be like
   if I was never born.
I hear singing.
I see colors.
I want to be a graphic designer.
I am odd and funny.

I pretend I can fly.
I feel like I'm burning inside.
I need peacefulness.
I worry that I won't lead a successful life.
I cry when one of my pets gets hurt.
I am odd and funny.

I understand I'm not perfect.
I say there is more than one world.
I dream about adventure.
I try to be strong.
I hope to be free from stress.
I am odd and funny.

Taylor Smith
Age: 10

DREAMS

The sky is a sea of dreams,
Holding onto everyone,
For if someone loses a dream,
That dream goes into the big blue sky.
If that dream doesn't find a way home,
That dream is taken to the black lake
Of the dying and dead dreams.

Kelsey N. Tarte
Age: 12

THE RHYTHM OF THE SEA

I stepped outside on a cold, stormy night,
The moon was calling to me.
The sea gulls yelled, their eyes shining bright,
I smelled the breath of the sea.
The hermit crabs danced to the beat of the waves,
As I sat all alone on the shore.
The dolphins laughed as they finished their games.
And they said, "That's the end; there's no more."
I went back inside to my warm, cozy bed.
I closed my eyes; shut them tight.
I dreamt about all the things I have said
And remembered that cold, stormy night.

Katie Dobscha
Age: 10

I AM WHO I AM

Sitting solemnly on the streets,
People walking around me, talking around me,
And sometimes singing around me,
Opening in the night, closing in the day,
I look at people walk down below me,
Things fly above just to show me,
That I am a Lamppost.

Paul Pemberton
Age: 11

THE STORM

Like a mad bull
The wind came crashing
Then the lightning came
Reaching down with long fingers
Its mission to rip apart the land
Thunder next sounded
Like a loud drum it sounded
All in all the storm was a monster
Trying to destroy the land
At last the sun breaks through the clouds
The storm retreats, its mission failed
But as it leaves it vows to come again

Theo Pratt
Age: 11

THE MOUNTAINS CALL

It was cold on the mountain.
It was like Old Man Winter
was blowing down my back
as I slid down the slippery slopes.
I felt like the mountain was my very own roller coaster
going in and out up and down
as I flew through the air
on nothing but a piece of wood.
The snow was like a bed of soft feathers
when I crashed
and the trees were like large men
trying to kill me as I tore down the mountainside.
The wind howled in my face
as I steadily went faster and faster.
The rain came then like a lion in the night.
Cold and wet it pored on my head
causing steam to rise from the snowy earth.
And then at the end of the day
I finally feel warmth as if it's been a thousand years.
I snuggle up in my bed. I never want to go.
But the call of the mountain is too strong for me
and I leave again the next day.

Jordan Fessenden
Age: 13

Fall

Fall looks like bare trees shedding their bark
   onto the ground.
Fall smells like ghosts and goblins at night
   playing tricks.
Fall tastes like candy
   spoiling little trick-or-treaters' dinner.
Fall feels like a slight breeze up against your neck
   when it is windy.
     Fall

Tristyn Catron
Age: 8

THE OLD HOUSE

An old house appeared.
Vines zigzagged up the cracked walls.
Its shutter's creak sounded like a frog
calling for a mate.
Its roof was a war zone.
Holes as big as five men were plentiful.
Tiny drops of water fell from the broken gutter
landing drip drop on the damp sidewalk.
With its yellowing paint and all the holes
the house was a block of Swiss cheese.
As I walked away I knew
that I would never forget that house.

Stephen Garfield
Age: 11

THANKSGIVING

Thank You
for all my hands can hold --
my cat when she's purring
because that's when she's most loving
and my flowers in my room that smell good.

Thank You
for all my eyes can see --
my mom and dad talking to me
and my trees in the fall.

Thank You
for all my ears can hear --
my tape player that my mom
turns on in the morning
and the birds chirping.

Shelby Rose Smith
Age: 7

BLUE

Blue is the color of the ocean
   that my dad takes me to.
Blue is the taste of fresh cotton candy
   from the fair.
Blue is the smell of blueberry pie
   fresh from the oven.
Blue is the color of my eyes
   when I look in the mirror.
Blue is the sound of a blue jay
   chirping in an apple tree.
Blue is my favorite color!

Alyssa Haney
Age: 9

BROWN

Brown sounds like horses running wild.
Brown tastes like freshly pealed grain.
Brown smells like silky horse skin.
Brown feels like dirt flying in the hair
   when a horse show is on.
Brown looks like branches running with the horses.

Shelby Brink
Age: 9

THE JOURNEY

There once were these horses who got along
They played and ran all day long
But then a mare got in their way
Bossing them around every day
She laid her ears back and yanked her head
Making them leave their grassy homestead
They roamed forests and mountains,
Deserts and plains
Galloping into London Lane
They left London quick as a flash
Arriving in Egypt where pyramids last
They saw the Great Sphinx and the Great Pyramid
Where tombs of rulers were buried and hid
They crossed a desert where the sand twirled
Sending it flying throughout the world
All of a sudden they hit a dead end
Standing still on a high cliff's bend
The horses took flight
And what a sight!
They flew back home with looks of pride
Ready to take their owners on a long ride.

Heather Arnold
Age: 12

MITCHELL M.

This is for the boy I once knew and passed away.
It's for the mom who wishes she could hear him say
"I love you"
Just one more day.
This is for the dad that says why did he have to
"die so young"?
It's for the brother that says I want you to
"Play with me"!
This is for all the people that knew this boy
We say we care, we say we're sorry
sad and confused of what you've done.
You may not have thought
you affected anyone here, but you did.
You affected
"everyone"!

Danielle Gunderson
Age: 12

WHITE

White sounds like the moving clouds.
White tastes like vanilla ice cream.
White smells like cotton candy.
White feels like a fluffy pillow.
White looks like a big piece of paper.

Jesse Swanstrom
Age: 9

Soundlessly gliding swift on a horse,
Existing together, earth seen never,
Trusting one another to onwardly stride,
Riding through dreams, real substance rather,
My body signals, my horse to slow.
Thick woods past, through fields onward to go,
Sword on my belt, shield at my side,
Battle cries sound, beating thorns in self-pride,
Speeding onward to life, sweet Savior inside.
Pleasures lie ahead, pleasures lie behind,
Yet today has calling, yearning daring adventure,
Whisper I to my soul, wander ever nearer,
The dear silver-wisdom, the quencher of souls.
Plowing grass soldiers, plights draw nigh,
Blankets of night, billowing sky,
Places to rest, plucked out of grasp,
Stormy silk clouds, seep deeper upon me.
Castles I pass, cathedral bells ring,
My eyes of lead, morning dawns nearer.
My horse I halt, mercy claimed favor,
Battles have ceased, beyond silent meadows.
All warriors gone home, accepting sweet victory,
Here will I rest. Here will I wait.
More battle cries draw me, the miracles still wait.

Charissa Joy Lugg
Age: 17

ALL FOR YOU

I'm sorry for all the things I did or didn't do...
I'm sorry for all the times I was not there for you.
I'm sorry for all the times I let you down...
For that I wish I was lost and could not be found.

I'm sorry...
I love you...

I'm sorry for all my friends...
They did not mean to offend.
I'm sorry if I misled.
I was trying to confess.

I'm sorry...
I love you...

I'm sorry for everything...
I will do anything.
For just one more chance...
So we could dance.

For all that with you...
You don't know what I would do.
Everything...
Just for you.

Luke Taylor
Age: 14

COLORS

Orange, black, yellow and green,
So many colors that I've never seen,
Purples and pinks, there are so many kinds,
I wonder what colors of blue I might find,
Tickle-me-pink, macaroni and cheese,
I've never seen colors as pretty as these,
Forest green, peach, teal and maroon,
Some of these colors are as bright as the moon,
Violet-blue and lemon and lime,
Too many colors and too little time,
Oh dear, oh my, I left out the red,
With so many colors I'm losing my head,
Magenta and gold and silver and gray,
There's no way I'll name all the colors today.

Levina Lynn Aberion
Age: 12

WHITE

White sounds like snowflakes falling from the sky.
White tastes like a snow cone when you take
a big bite out of it.
White smells like the fresh mountain air.
White feels like a snow dove's white feathers.
White looks like the white and fluffy clouds.

Bronsun J. Severns
Age: 9

OF MICE, RATS... AND YOU!

Wild
they sit small and fat
eating little morsels
that did not belong to them.
by day they scurry away
too timid to face an unknown world
in which roamed fierce leviathans.

Tame
they crouch upon a shoulder
sniffing in endearing affection
at an ear, pattering on a desk
gazing with tiny eyes
in rapt attention into your face
past eyes and skin
and into your heart.
they disappear
leaving you enthralled, to find
they have woven your hair
with the care of an artisan
into a hammock, to swing with
closed eyes above the shoulder
of that which is all their world,
around which the dawn is rising.

Caitlin Hardee
Age: 11

GREEN

Green is like a tree on top of a hill and grass.
Green is like a taste of a kiwi on a hot summer day.
Green is like the water making wavy sounds.
Green is like the green light on the road.
Green is like seaweed in the water.

Jana M. Danielak
Age: 10

RED

Red is as red as hot steaming lava.
Red is as tasty as liquorice.
Red is as tasty as a strawberry
   with whipped cream on it.
Red reminds me of eating Reeses' Pieces
   and red M&M's.
Red reminds me of a rug burn.

John A. Bardwell
Age: 10

RELIGIONS

At the dawn of time faiths have bloomed,
Some religions are bound to be doomed,

Egyptian mythology, long dead for a while,
To the gods they thank the flooding of the Nile,
With gods like Amun-Re, Osiris, and Seth,
Isis, Horus, Anubis, god of death,

Greek mythology, Greece's traditional religion,
Socrates' philosophy and this faith had a collision,
Many years later they gave up their faith,
Knowing it was naive,
Another religion they must believe,

Shinto, still practiced today,
To gods like Amaterasu, sun goddess they pray,
"Way of the Kami", spirits in rocks, rivers, and trees,
In mountains, animals, rivers, and the breeze,

There's Judaism, they honor one God,
Their symbols, Star of David, and Jessie's Rod,
Jews honor Christ as a prophet, not our Lord,
This man of peace doesn't carry a sword,

Taoism, a belief of Chinese,
A philosophy,
Like what was taught by Confucius and Socrates,
The spiritual order of nature it stresses,
But sometimes this order can get into messes,

Hinduism, their lives in a wheel,
Through reincarnation, their "wounds" they must heal,
With karma and dharma in their daily lives,
And meat, they mustn't eat and kill
With weapons like knives,

Buddhism, based on nonviolence, charity, compassion,
With many a monks, orange robes are their fashion,
Nirvana, they must all achieve,
And Gautama Buddha, the first one they believe,

Islam, to Allah, our God, they pray,
In town you see Muslims, praying each day,
There are different sects, some more extreme,
Some group as terrorists, and work as a team,

Christians, we honor Jesus
As the "beginning and end,"
He died to save us, and will come again,
Christ taught us to love one another,
And to help each and every "sister and brother,"

At the end of time, the world in destruction,
Let's see who has made the right deduction,
Maybe the Christians, the Rapture, the abduction,
Or maybe the Hindus, Shiva's earth reconstruction,

All these religions, so special, unique,
We must all pick one to seek,
Because if you don't have a religion
You've missed out a lot,
Put your faith into something people have taught,
So many of them, not understood,
So before you choose, learn them, if you would.

Joseph Drouin
Age: 12

SMILES

Smiles go miles and miles and miles
and never end up in piles.
They can be on kitchen tiles
or in grocery store aisles.
But trust me, I say, they go miles.

Camille Jean Brown
Age: 8

A SWIMMER

I am a competitive girl who loves to swim.
I wonder if someday
I will become an Olympic medal winner.
I hear the hush of the crowd
when the United States flag is flown.
I see the circular gold medal placed around my neck.
I want to feel the pure pleasure of my victory.
I am a competitive girl who loves to swim.

I pretend I am slicing into still as glass water
to begin the race.
I feel the excitement as I look behind me
and see my opponent.
I anticipate the rough cement of the end of the pool.
I cry as I realize all my hard work is over.
I worry if it all was a waste.
I am a competitive girl who loves to swim.

I understand now the feeling of being the best.
I say a quick prayer of thankfulness.
I dream of all that is to come.
I believe I can do anything if I try.
I hope someday to reach the finish line.
I am a competitive girl who loves to swim.

Brooke Kerr
Age: 17

FRIENDS... FOREVER?

I once had a friend
Who said she'd be there
'Til the end.
But she wasn't.
Now, this is a tale
Of a friendship
That was doomed to fail.
I met her on the first
Day of preschool.
She shared her toys
And said I was pretty cool.
Every day, we played
And played and played and played.
She said we were best friends,
And that our friendship would never fade.
We spent days at each other's house,
Only to beg to stay
Longer and longer and longer
But our parents would say,
"It's time to go, maybe another day."
We would sadly say our good-byes
And trudge homeward.
Eventually, my family had to move.
When I came forward
To tell her,
All she wanted to know is why,
Why could such a thing occur?
We hugged and wondered,
Why were friendships torn apart?
Oh, I was so confused.
When it came time for us to part,
We were both in tears.

Tears streaming down her face,
She said, "We're still friends forever."
I could see that there was a trace
Of doubt on her face.
Now, years later, I wonder,
Are we still friends?
And, as I blunder,
"No, of course not,"
My mom tells me I got a letter.
It's from her.
And I felt better
As I read the letter.

Now I am not so doubtful,
That a friendship can last forever,
No matter how far stretched
No matter how far stressed
No matter how hopeless you get,
There will always be that person
Who came into your life
And left footprints in your heart.

Allison Rutherford
Age: 13

IMAGINE THAT

Up a sunny windowpane;
Down a rushing water drain.
Sometimes something of no explanation;
Maybe a land of my own creation.
Scuba-diving in the deep blue sea;
Buzzing with a fuzzy bumblebee.
Reciting lovely poetry and prose;
Snorting the alphabet with my nose.
Making an animal of my own;
Turning my enemy into stone.
Drinking the ocean in one big gulp;
Squishing a rock right into pulp.
Cleaning the world with a feather duster;
Telling the wind not to blow nor bluster.
Painting a picture with no paints just paper;
Solving the mystery of the unicorn caper.
Driving a great big ocean liner;
Being a gold or silver miner.
Exploring a boarded up, haunted ghost mansion;
Directing a New York Highway expansion,
Doing anything as I desire;
Wow, my imagination on fire!

Katy Westlund

SUMMER

Hot sun in the air
Cool breeze going by
A ball in the sky
What a delight
Oh how much fun it is.

Tim Walden
Age: 13

STORM

A storm,
Is an angry giant,
That bellows at the earth,
And when it rains softly,
It's lots of little fairies,
Tickling your nose.

Ericka Smith

GREEN

green is the color of grass
green is the color of leaves
green is the color of my pencil
green is the color of trees
green is the color of our couch

Kevin Ruiz
Age: 9

A TEAR FOR DREAMS

So
sad a
sorrow one
has but had,
about a happy
dream. To watch it
fade, and take flight,
upon its golden wings.
The misery which then sets
in, and fills the vacant void, is
not but tears and empty hearts
searching for some joy. Will it be
found? We pray it might, or happiness
will die. So keep your golden
dreams in sight, even
when you cry.

Karin Lewis
Age: 16

COOL NIGHT'S MIST

A forest of dark skeletons tower over
an icy mountain stream.
Salmon make their yearly run
across its bed of rock.
Crisp golden leaves whirl on the ground
like a blanket flapping in the wind.
Thick gray clouds dance across
the face of the moon,
its glow cast eerie, black shadows
over the forest floor.
Like the moon's light, an owl's call fades
with the cool night's mist.

Liz Nelson
Age: 14

GREEN

Green sounds like the lemon by your ears.
Green tastes like a limey taste in the air.
Green smells like a lemon lime smell in your nose.
Green feels like holding a kiwi.
Green looks like the green grass blowing in the wind.

Dylan Minogue
Age: 9

WINTER

Winter sounds like a quiet universe.
Winter tastes like vanilla ice cream as I eat it up.
Winter smells like a newly born fluffy rabbit.
Winter feels like my cozy soft dog.
Winter looks like snowflakes falling on my nose.

Anne Erho
Age: 9

THE RIVER

The river races
like wild horses
Water crashing against rocks
like lightning
in the black night sky
River water
as cold as the snow
that blankets the branches
of the trees

Kara Dunn
Age: 12

MY LITTLE SISTERS

My little sisters are messy and clean
    but I still love them.
My little sisters are short and tall
    but I still love them.
My little sisters are grumpy and sweet
    but I still love them.
My little sisters have blond and brown hair
    but I still love them.
My little sisters have green and blue eyes
    but I still love them.
My little sisters are hyper and calm
    but I still love them.
My little sisters sleep with me
    but I still love them.
My little sisters are cute and funny
    but I still love them.
My little sisters are scared of the dark
    but I still love them.
My little sisters fight with me
    but I still love them.
My little sisters are scared of bugs
    but I will always love them.

Kayla Meischke
Age: 9

AUTUMN

Lavish colors, scarlet, orange, and brown,
Freezing gusts of wind whipping 'round.
Hoarfrost sparkling over the yard,
People receiving their first Christmas card.
Thankful good people breaking some bread,
Crackly, dead leaves blowing over my head.
Cups of spice cider or piping hot cocoa,
Humming a tune ever so slow.
Cheery warm fires and cozy warm blankets,
Spending your evenings
Watching beautiful sunsets.
Raking up piles of fallen, dry leaves,
Kids messing them up, one of your pet peeves.
The season is lovely, no matter the weather,
Next will come snow, light as a feather.

Sarah E. Bernier
Age: 12

MY TEACHER

My teacher is smart.
My teacher is pretty.
My teacher is nice.
My teacher is the best teacher in the world
And that is why I like her!

Haley Sherman
Age: 10

MY LITTLE ONE

Look at her smile laughing with glee,
As she cozies up like a small warm bear,
Making me smile when she smiles at me,
I smell the scent that comes off her hair,
Smells like an infant straight from heaven,
With the skin color of the perfect chocolate mix,
It's almost her birthday she's on month seven,
Almost my birthday too I'm soon to be six,
Her chubby cheeks like the color of rose,
Her stubby legs kick but it's obvious she's glad,
She swings her arms when I tickle her toes,
The memory was sweet but it kind of looked sad,
For the lights were gloomy, dark in the room,
Giving me a weird face after I kissed her,
Her belly looks like a tiny full moon,
I expressed my love for my sister.

Aaron Caleb Toves
Age: 15

WOLFIE

Wolfie is my great cat
She is definitely not fat
She loves to go outside and play
She stays out there almost all day
She loves catching birds and mice
But she is really very nice
Wolfie is black and brown
She's always acting like a clown
She has a long, bushy tail
It looks like a boat with its sail
Wolfie has long brown fur
She's never cold, having to think brrr!
She loves sleeping by the fireplace at night
It really is such a cute sight
Wolfie really likes to eat
She's really messy, not neat
Wolfie doesn't like the cold
Maybe because she's five years old
She loves to play with her cat toys
Some of them make quite a loud noise
Wolfie plays and gets frisky
This behavior is very risky
She loves scratching on her post
It's the toy she likes the most
Wolfie is skinny and small
She looks like a little ball
She loves catnip very much
I only give her the slightest touch
Wolfie hates getting bathed and groomed
As if it were though she was doomed
When Wolfie's hungry, she always meows
It's her was of saying "I want it now!"

Wolfie likes to stare at my fish
She wants to eat it, that's her wish
Wolfie is the greatest cat
I'll love her always and that's that

Emily Brown
Age: 12

Fall
Fall looks like it's raining with all the leaves
    falling on the ground.
Fall smells like freshly baked cookies
    and freshly carved pumpkins.
Fall tastes like yummy, crunchy candy
    and caramel apples.
Fall feels like a chilly snow.
    You can fall it is so slippery.
        Fall

Thomas N. DeSuler
Age: 8

I like to rhyme
My name is Boe,
But look at the time
I have to go.

Tyler Kamp
Age: 10

THANKSGIVING

Thank You
for all my hands can hold --
a friendly puppy
and my blanket that is spotted
with color.

Thank You
for all my eyes can see --
colors in the world, maybe bright
or not, and a smile on the faces
of my family.

Thank You
for all my ears can hear --
a song that makes my ears twitch,
but in a tune that is very happy,
and the waves crashing against a rock.

Natalie Smith
Age: 7

Friends
cool, fun
talk, play, run
caring, listening, laughing, encouraging
Girls

Kristina Biggs
Age: 9

THE CAT

Prowling, hunting, catching, chasing
It's the cat
Prowling through the house
ears so sensitive to hear a mouse.
It's the cat
stalking, running, cornering, eating
climbing up to view its pray running
and catching through the under brush
never stopping for very much
the heart of the rodent has stopped
the cat has pounced into the jaws of terror
the rodent cannot see
as it is blinded by its own fear!!!
Only one name can cover this
beautiful and graceful beast...
Cat

Amy Rose Hodge
Age: 10

C aring Father
H onest and truthful
R ight on things
I ntelligent and smart
S etting an example
T eaching others

Cali Mandak
Age: 9

MY GRANDMA

My grandma is a nice,
and kind grandma,
Sometimes when I visit her,
she bakes my favorite, cookies.
The cookies she baked,
for me is chocolate chip,
When I smell it,
it smells like creaming chocolate,
and sweet,
My grandma likes to,
tell me stories of her,
childhood and legends,
When I have dinner,
with my grandma,
she makes crisping chicken,
green beans, and spice chicken noodles,
That's why I like my grandma.

Juile Vang

Michael
Fun
Jumping on trampoline and playing football
He makes me laugh
Speedy

Nickolas Olson
Age: 9

J asmine likes 'NSYNC
A nd the Backstreet Boys.
S he listens to it a lot.
M y sister is cool
I n a way
N ice to me
E very day.

Andrew Daniel Marcus Clark

MY DOG

My dog's name is Haru.
She really likes to chew.
She chews on toys and boys.
I really get annoyed with her.
She chews on my kittens and my mittens,
But I love her still.

Chelsey Aragon
Age: 10

WHEN I LOOK OUT THE WINDOW

When I look out the window
I see a tower,
When it rains it takes a shower.
When I look out the window,
I see Puget Sound,
It is shaped sort of round.
When I look out the window
I see Mt. Rainier,
I think I just spotted a deer.
When I look out the window
I see a dark night,
But it looks better by the moonlight.

Tommy Corwin
Age: 10

MY SISTER

My sister is always there for me.
Even if I'm being mean.
Sometimes it feels like she doesn't like me.
But after all she's done for me
I know she's going to be here for me.

Caitlyn Johnson
Age: 10

MY SKATEBOARD

Santa Cruz decks brake intensely in the crisp air.
Lucky seven bearings pound roughly
On the slick ground.
Spitfire wheels spin fast during manuals.
Independent trucks grind smoothly on silver rails.
But I skateboard softly on steep ramps.

Cody Jensen
Age: 10

SPORTS

We are all sitting watching the game
And we all want the ball gone, gone, gone
Way out there and the MARINERS to win.
Again and again!!!
The crowd roars as I sip my soda
And eat my hot dog and peanuts.

Brad Norman
Age: 10

AT MIDNIGHT

At midnight I sing
A song. If I do, it's for
My pleasure.

It may be very clever
In the moon I see
A star. I see it from
Near and far.

I love that star
With all my might
And I will wish upon
That star tonight.

Erika McGrady
Age: 10

CALIFORNIA TO WASHINGTON

Driving from California is a thrill!
Everything amazingly beautiful
Dried from the heat
In the middle part of California,
Things are greener.
Oregon,
Green hills that you go between.
Washington,
Good old Washington,
Fur trees that are as green can be!
How did they all get that way?
Colors all mixed together
Take time to notice
California to Washington
Everything is beautiful!

Gracie Newman
Age: 10

CHRISTMAS

Christmas is a time of cheer,
Christmas is a giving time of the year,
We give our families lots of joys
With presents and toys.

Jordan Stephens
Age: 10

FAIRIES IN THE MEADOW

When the fairies celebrate
O'r in the meadow there
The kings and queens and other great
Dance without a care

This party lasts all night
When all people sleep
They eat to their heart's content
Then go home without a peep

I know this because one night
When I was bound for home
A light in the meadow beckoned
And I knew I wasn't alone

Andrea Fahmy
Age: 10

ROLL AWAY TIME

Today I sit on a hill
near the bay
watching time roll away
I sit there all day
until night comes
and day has flown away

Ian Stark
Age: 10

HELP

Help us Lord, please help us
We need to know you're here
We need to seek your persistence
I need to hear you in my ear

Those are the words that people said
Just back on 9-11
Lord why did you let this happen?
Why couldn't we just have fun?

"My children," God said looking down
"Please do not dispute
For all that I have given you
Is a blessing in disguise."

All I did was use my powers
I just knocked down two precious Towers
I did not knock out your food supply
I did not let you perish and die

"Oh yeah!" said everybody
"We're stronger in the Lord"
For we did not get killed
When terrorists tried our peace to destroy
But all they did was build.

Nicholas Phillips
Age: 11

GREEN

Green is my favorite color.
Green is the color of trees.
I like to climb trees
Because it's so much fun.
I rake the leaves,
I go up in the trees,
And jump off
And land in leaves.

Mitchell Cole
Age: 9

A timeless waltz of gentle summer breeze,
The whisper of the autumn's early snow;
The dusty sunlight sifting through the trees,
The plodding of the tidal ebb and flow;
A budding leaf, the misty rains of spring,
The jagged cliff sides, sweeping plains below;
The glory sun, and warmth it brings,
The teeming sea, the mountains capped with snow --
All these created, formed from formlessness,
And molded by the loving hands of One
Who spoke forth life and light from emptiness,
And having given thus, He gave His Son,
   Who bore for us our sin and pain and scorn,
   And rose again, that we might be reborn.

Gabriel Stephen Weber
Age: 17

RAINBOW COLORS

Red is the color
Of a big apple,
Orange is the color
Of a juicy orange.
Yellow is the color
Of a ripe banana,
Green is the color
Of yummy spinach.
Blue is the color
Of blue Kool-Aid.
Indigo is the color
Of my dinner plate.
Violet is the color
Of a bowlful of grapes.

Kayla Holguin
Age: 8

FRED

There once was a hamster named Fred,
Who couldn't get out of his bed,
He was so fat,
He looked like a cat,
He couldn't get into the shed.

Micaela Fagan
Age: 10

BUTTERFLY

Looking as hard as I can through leaves,
I found something!
It felt like a breeze,
So I looked around.
I sneaked out and caught it.
Then I saw it was the most beautiful thing,
A butterfly.

Amy Handlan
Age: 8

WINTER SPARKLES LEAD TO SPRING

Winter comes and hears a harp,
I decide it's best to play it.
I learn a song,
And play a concert,
But a few days later,
Is the last night of winter.
I make a snowman,
The night is here,
The snowman melts
And spring is here.
My flowers come,
Now that smells good.
Oh thank goodness spring is here.

Kathryn Sayre
Age: 8

CHOCOLATE

C andy
H eavenly taste
O h so delish
C ookies and cream
O ne of my favorite types of candy
L uxurious taste
A bsolutely the best kind of chocolate is milk chocolate
T asteful flavor
E xtremely mouth-watering!

Kara McCarty

S kateboarding through the skate park.
K icking the board to do an ollie.
A fter I fall I get back up again.
T asting the ground as I fall!
E veryone cheering me on.
B ack on the ground I go.
O UCH!!
A nother fall
R oaring laughter.
D oing daring tricks.
I finally land something!
N ever will I fall again!!
G oing back to home for rest.

Chris Looney

War
awful terrible
fighting dying killing
rage anger thankfulness trust
caring loving giving
great wonderful
Peace

Sydne Phillips
Age: 10

PETS

Some are fuzzy and cute
And some are mean and rude.
Some pets purr, some bark, some squeak.
Some even hiss and snarl.
Some pets are rough and cuddly,
But the one pet I love most is my cat Charlie.

Alannah Carlson
Age: 11

SOUNDS

Sounds are all around
High sounds or low
Sounds that are sweet
Or sounds that give you a creep
They may sound like a swallow's chirp
Or a hippo's burp
A mouse's peep
And a neigh of a sheep
Sounds are everywhere

Dalton Darmody
Age: 10

MY FAVORITE ANIMAL

Do you know my favorite animal?
It is very fun!
Well is it one that can run?
Can it jump or leap?
Maybe curl itself in a heap?
Is it a cat or a dog?
Does it feel like a frog?
Can it wear a hat or is it extremely fat?
Or is it tall or short?
Does it run on a basketball court?
Well, my favorite animal is pretty funky
Because he is a monkey!

Lauren Komarzec
Age: 10

COFFEE

C offee is a good way to wake up.
O nly have one cup a day.
F un to drink the foam.
F or some people it has too much caffeine.
E ach gulp is better than the other.
E very cup is good.

Lisa Creatura

STICKS AND STRINGS
MAKE WONDERFUL DREAMS

You hold the guitar and I hold the sticks,
   together we pump out some pretty cool licks.
I play my drums, I play 'em really hard.
   You're up front with your strings standing guard.
We rock really fast, we roll really slow.
   If we try really hard we can make some dough.
With a few simple notes
   and some well-chosen words,
    we can be more than a couple of nerds.

Everyone loves us and our band is hot,
   our producer says we've hit the jackpot.
The playin' feels good and the tours are fun,
   the fans scream and shout 'til the concert is done!

Austin A. Hershman

Earth's life
Ensuring an abundance of wondrous sensations,
Stroll the waterfront,
Glimpsing magnificent sunsets,
Wind breezing through your hair,
Perceiving God's cosmos
Gyrating around the place
We love to dub,
Earth

Holly Warter
Age: 13

COLORS

I love big red sleds in January,
Pink valentines and white lace in February,
Green shamrocks in March,
Blue jays in April,
Yellow buttercups in May,
Purple violets in June,
Silver fireworks in July,
Indigo water beneath the bridge in August,
Golden leaves falling from trees in September,
Orange jack-o'-lanterns on fence posts in October,
Brown turkeys in November,
And white snow falling in the mountains
In December.

Emily Kathryn Roberts
Age: 8

THE OCEAN

The ocean sparkling in the morning sun,
Going home when the day is done,
Memories of my special day,
My family together just to play.
Boats going in and out,
Of harbors as the sailors shout,
Sea gulls fight over bread crumbs,
Listening to the bumblebees hum.
This has been a delightful place,
You can tell by the smile on my face.

Maureen Tremblay
Age: 9

MOONLIGHT SKY

Moonlight sky
In the night,
The stars are shining bright.
And in the distance
I can almost see --
Yes, yes...
I can see Mercury.
The sun is coming up,
The moon is going down.
It is breakfast time,
But I can't hear a sound.

Erin Elizabeth Smith
Age: 8

RAINBOW

R ed is the color of delicious sweet apples,
O range is the color of a juicy good orange,
Y ellow is the color of the hot sun,

G reen is the color of freshly mowed grass,

B lue is the color of a clear sky,
I ndigo is the color of storm clouds,
V iolet is the color of roses growing in our garden.

Ryan Smith
Age: 8

All of creation that surrounds me rings
The wonders, praise, and glories of my King.
He made the earth on its foundation stand,
And waters covered it at His command.
At His rebuke and thunder waters fled
And flowered o'er mountains and ravines instead.
He is the Lord of bright day and black night.
He manages the sun and the moon for light
Both man and beast alike to God do cry
For He their hunger and thirst will supply.
Though plants may wither and seas may drain,
The glories of God forever remain.
So fear not nature, nor revere its might;
Serve God, like earth, and tremble in His sight.

Christina Haass
Age: 16

ICE CREAM

Ice cream, ice cream,
Can't be beat,
And cookie dough is
The best to eat!
That's my favorite
Under the sun,
When it melts,
It makes me all sticky,
But I don't mind,
It's still my favorite kind.

Molly Deutsch
Age: 8

I'VE GOT FAITH IN GOD

It wasn't just some pieces of glass
It wasn't just a building
It is gone but I will always remember this day

Lots of people have died this day
But don't let your trust in Him go away
Be strong with faith
For the Lord will help us win the battle

I am sad
But I have faith in the Lord

Daniel Hendrickson
Age: 8

YELLOW

Yellow is the color of the sun
On a summer day,
Of wheat swaying in the wind
In spring.
Yellow is the color of leaves in autumn,
And the color of glowing eggnog
On a winter night.

Leo Clerc
Age: 8

Stands there the lily clothed in splend'rous white,
Adorned in grace, arrayed in garments bright
And steeped in beauty -- oh! so rich and fare,
That crowned kings in purple robes look bare,
When next this simple flower of the field;
Which in the ground lay covered and concealed,
Just six short weeks ago, 'til sun and rain
Did cause`its seed to grow and bloom again.
Stands there the lily -- flower of Nature born?
No, God the lily made and does adorn
In yet more dazzling dress and sweet perfume,
Than God-created man can e'er assume.
    Then come; oh come extol the Lord with me,
    Our God, to whom all praise and glory be.

Sharalyn Bechtel
Age: 17

GREEN

Green is the color of a forest.
It is the color of a swamp.
When I think of green,
I think of moss on the trees.
Green is the color of seaweed
And the sea.
It is the color of poison ivy.
It is the color of a leaf
During the spring.

Brenden Youtsler
Age: 8

COLORS OF BIRDS

Blue is the color of stellar jays,
Bluebirds, blue jays, and indigo buntings.

Red is the color of cardinals, acorn woodpeckers,
Ruby-crowned kinglets, and scarlet tanagers.

Yellow is the color of orange-crowned warblers,
Yellow warblers, townsend's warblers,
And American goldfinches.

Black is the color of American crows, ravens,
Blackbirds, and red-winged blackbirds.

Connor Smith
Age: 8

C an it be Christmas Eve?
H appy warm feeling inside.
R acing for presents.
I feel excited I am.
S anta is coming down the chimney.
'T is the season to be jolly.
M ay it be Christmas Eve?
A cheerful night.
S omebody turn on the Christmas lights!

Christmas

Chelsie Sablan

WINTER

Winter is cold,
Winter is white,
Winter, winter, winter is tonight.

Winter is icy,
Winter is snowy,
Winter, winter, winter is tonight.

Winter is nice,
Winter is fun,
Winter, winter, winter is tonight.

Elizabeth E. Ewing
Age: 9

B eagles running at great speeds through the yard
E ating the green grass along the way
A cting as a fox silently sneaking through the plain
G rowing and chasing the quick squirrels
    fast and furiously
L ooking anxiously for an unusual spot to bury her bone
E ars flapping up and down trying to catch a bird
S itting at the door banging her claws
    against the glass telling me to let her in

Scott Benedict

GYMNASTICS

G ymnastics is a wonderful sport
Y et there is judging on all
M any events like beam, floor, uneven bars
    and vault make up a meet
N ow here come the gymnasts doing flips and back tucks
A riels, front handsprings, and cartwheels
    on a four-inch wide beam
S pringing up, up, up on a springboard
T wisting off the vaulting horse
I nteresting routines
C ertainly there is not another sport like this one
S trength and flexibility is the key to winning first,
    there is no sport like gymnastics

Stephanie Atchison
Age: 10

PAINT DROPS

It is this time of year once again
when the world turns red and orange.
I look out the window and what do I see?
I see paintbrushes that look rather crooked to me.
The colors on them are red and orange paint
dripping rapidly to the ground.

The paint looks as if they are dancing in the air
until they touch the ground.
When the globs of paint fall in a pile,
children run outside and jump into the pile
of red and orange paint.
The strange thing is the paint does not stick.

Maybe the paintbrushes are branches of a tree
and the paints are just leaves.
Maybe, just maybe,
everything just looks strange to me.

Heide Luong
Age: 10

Earth is sublime
Looks peaceful as creatures wander silently
Smells like forest pine in snowy mountains
Feels like a sauna across a windy desert
Sounds like waves crashing over a rocky beach
Earth is magnificent

Zach Howe
Age: 13

TABLES AND CHAIRS

Why are tables here?
They have four legs but they don't walk or talk?
They store stuff, but can't hold more stuff?
Why can't chairs be man's best friend?
My thoughts never end.
Do chairs have hairs?
Can chairs hold mares?
Have you heard of double-decker tables?
Why can't they have labels?
I love tables.
I have a table in my stable,
With a bear on my chair, eating a pear.
Oh my chair.
This is not fair.
I want my chair.

Mac E. Powell
Age: 10

MY FRIEND LAUREN

Playing wall ball together and laughing so hard
that the ball bounces off someone's head.
Talking on the phone so long
that my mom had to get me off.
Trying to be quiet and end up laughing
so no one could concentrate.
That's what friends are for.

Jordyn Panitzke
Age: 10

WINTER WONDERLAND

As I play in the winter wonderland
I remember last summer when I played in the sand.
Now I play in the winter, not spring, summer or fall.
I frolic in the snow and that's all.
Okay maybe I played with my blue ball.
Okay maybe that's not all.
In the fall I played on my sled.
Now I'm getting tucked into bed.

But wait, that was all a dream.
What a scheme in my mind with the sand
in the land in the winter wonderland.

Alena Noson
Age: 11

S liding on the powdery snow.
N ever will I quit.
O ff the jump, a nice view.
W inding through the trees
B anging the snow off my board.
O ver the hills while cold wind blows gently
   across my face.
A lways faster and faster.
R acing toward the finish line.
D oing a daring flip.
I taste the snow as I fall.
N ice flip my friend said.
G oing to do it again next winter.

Soleil Clerc

BUSY CITY

Today I went to see the busy city down in the sea.
The busy city is full of creatures
That are different shapes and sizes.
A school of fish looks as if they're cars in traffic.
The coral is like big working towers and skyscrapers.
Whales remind me of jets soaring through the ocean.
And I'm here to explore the wonders of the sea.

Chelsee Bertelsen
Age: 10

SEASONS

Winter, fall, spring, and summer,
These are all the seasons.
In the winter there's snow galore
That's cold across my cheek.
In the fall where there are leaves
Falling from the trees,
I just love the colors on those leaves.
In the spring the trees are blossoming,
Pink and white with color.
In the summer the sun is blazing,
Down on everyone.
I really like the seasons,
And now my poem is done.

Grace Chakerian
Age: 8

WOLF

When I look out my bedroom
I see a creature of the night
a wolf solemnly howling at the moon
when I look he stares at me
with his big yellow eyes
full of mysteries and questions

Kaitlyn M. Savage
Age: 11

CLOUDS

There are clouds in the sky
Drifting ever so high
They're formed and broken, formed and broken
Swirling through the chilly breeze
Formed and broken, formed and broken
Floating through the cloudy seas
Formed and broken, formed and broken
Gliding and whirling past the sun
Formed and broken, formed and broken
The life of a cloud must be a peaceful one
Formed and broken, formed and broken

Natalie Morningstar
Age: 10

THANK YOU GOD FOR ME

Thank you God for me
Thank you for my neighbors
And my friends and my family
THANK YOU GOD FOR ME

Gibby Guest
Age: 9

CAITLYN

Caitlyn,
Active,
Whisk past me in a whirl of gold,
Like a leaf in the wind,
Jumping flinging in the air,
Knocking into one another,
Collapsing into the grass,
Swimming chasing into the bay,
Smelling like the sea,
Time for walking she knows,
Sniffing every leaf along the way,
Sticking her head in dirty mud puddles to drink,
Disappointment when we start turning home,
Time for puppy kisses,
Begging for treats,
So sweet

Veronica Leigh Winget
Age: 10

WINSTON

I have a friend,
He is small and gray.
Even though he is old,
He brightens my day.
He doesn't play much now,
But he is still boss of the house.
He's not very quick,
But he can still catch a mouse.
He does not make friends,
Like he did in the past.
He gets a little scared, but this won't last.
He stays in the house most of the day,
He likes to sleep later,
Then play,
He does not like to go out,
But stays in instead,
If he won't come when you call,
Look under the bed.

Evan Tremblay
Age: 9

A BAD DAY

My grandma forgot to wake me up.
I woke up at 8:49.
I forgot to do my hair.
I looked like a blob.
I didn't know what to do.
I rushed unlike ever.
I called my mom.
She said that it was up to me.
I had to work hard, hard, hard.
I was so late I didn't go to school.

Coltin Hardy
Age: 8

MY MONSTER

I have a hairy pet monster
His name is El Fredo de Hauntster
He likes to eat small toys
Sometimes fat little boys

' Hauntster looks like goopy tar
He's strong enough to crush a car
He takes the time to play in rocky rubbles
And he's really good at blowing big bubbles

By the way, he really likes to play dice
And loves to cuddle with small mice
In fact, he has a pet one named Cory
But that's an entirely different story!

Brad Andrews
Age: 11

Open me
I am a door
I see people's lives
I watch over them
I help them with hellos

Close me
I am a door
I watch the sick
I watch them suffer
I help them with good-byes

Open or close me
I am a door
You can do whatever you want to me
You command me

Close me
I am a door
Good-bye

Andy Osborn
Age: 13

SHE WAS ONLY THIRTEEN

She was so thin,
But in her mind she just didn't fit in.
She looked at her reflection,
And felt a strong sense of rejection.
Day-by-day,
She slowly began to fade away.
She looked so thin and pale.
She used to be so strong.
How did she become so frail?
She was in so much pain,
Yet it was all in vain.
I remember the telephone call.
They said they couldn't save her,
They said she had become too small.
I couldn't believe that she was really dead,
She looked so lifeless on that hospital bed.
As I stood by her grave,
I felt so unbrave.
I wondered how I would make it
Through life without her.
Everything soon began to blur,
And my only thoughts were of her.
Things are rough -- but I live day-to-day,
I just can't help but wonder
Why my little angel had to go away.
O' God, why couldn't she stay?

Bethany MacLay
Age: 13

THE WONDERFUL SEASONS

Spring is here,
a fawn is born,
the squirrel is out, a bear wakes up,
the farmer plants his garden,

For summer is already here,
the fawn walks fine now,
the squirrel is fat,
the bear had its cubs,
the birds have their chicks,
the farmer picks his food,

Fall is finally here,
the fawn has its horns,
the squirrel stocks up,
the bear gets nice and fat,
the birds fly south,
the farmer freezes his food,

Winter is here,
the fawn is living on its own,
the squirrel is in its home,
the bear is asleep,
the birds are south,
the farmer is eating his food,

Spring is here again,
and the cycle begins again.

Marlee Metcalf
Age: 9

TRAMPOLINES HURT PEOPLE TOO

Angel-like, you soar through the air.
Almost the same as a fan, the air flies into your face.
Arms spread like an airplane.
Then thrusted in front of you like an Olympic diver.
Crunch, like two cars colliding into each other
at sixty miles per hour on the freeway,
you hit the ground.
The pain reminds you
of a thousand needles piercing your skin.

You wake up; the pain has dulled
but still hurts like you are a baseball
and the batter just hit a home run.
You're lying on the ground
like a helpless turtle on its back.
Only thing you can see is the hard cement.
When you stand up, you get lightheaded
like there's someone pumping you up
like a basketball.
Then your throat tightens
like someone stretched it out.

You wander into the house,
searching for your mother.
Like a drifting balloon you float through the rooms.
When you find her, you look up with big eyes
the same as a puppy dog does,
and then scrunch your nose up.
You take a deep breath and say,
"We're gettin' rid of the trampoline."

Andrew VanLierop - DeGoede
Age: 13

PUPPY DOG

Puppy
cute fun
cuddling winning wrestling
bone chewy toy basket food
chasing barking running
fast cute
Dog

Becca Whaley

TREES

Trees
They are beautiful wonders.
Brown leaves, red ones, yellow ones, and green.
Trees have bees on them.

Trees are getting cut down,
That's cutting down our oxygen.
Please don't cut them down...
Please.

Trees are amazing.
So please don't cut them down.
Trees they are beautiful wonders,
Trees!

Gaven S. Ayala
Age: 11

FRIENDS

you
have a friend
that friend is me
we stand together
through rain and
shine
we stand together through
all rough times
you have a friend
a very good friend
you have
a friend
that friend is
me

Ali Worley
Age: 10

Fear and grief, sorrow and pain
Beloved ones gone insane
Simple rules like love thy brother
Like a match we begin to smother

More villains than we can afford
Now strike a fateful, eerie death chord
Wars spread widely across the planet
So intense I cannot stand it

But there is hope shining bright before us
We can join the goodly chorus
We can do our best and try
To end the turmoil, to justify

Forgive your foes of wrongs and sins
In most cases the good guy wins
If there is something we can do
It's join together; it starts with you.

Karlan Hansen
Age: 12

M arvelous
O utstanding
T eaches me
H elps me
E xcellent
R emembering

F amous
A mazing
T eaches me
H elps me
E xciting
R eally cool

Samuel W. Lakin
Age: 9

C arefully laying eggs
R eady to be fried for lunch
A trocious smelling when dead
Y ummy when barbecued
F un to watch
I ntelligent little animals
S wimming backwards with their tails
H appy to be alive!

Clint V. Lieseke
Age: 10

FIRST

I'm a star in cool night's air.
I wait for my friends but they're not there.
I'm standing here all alone,
I just stand here cold as a bone.
No moon, I'm the only light,
I guess I'm the first star out tonight.

Monica Domena
Age: 9

THOUGHTS OF AN AMERICAN SOUL

A beautiful country under siege
Will it fall upon its knees?
No, for 'tis America
Dreams tinted in red, white, and blue

Now war has commenced
The traitors will not get away
Even though who did this crime
Is really hard to say.

We will rise again
For we will take none captured
Ten wins will not suffice
For we are Americans, with hearts unbeatably pure!

Kelsey Jarone
Age: 10

WINTER

Snowflakes in the sky.
Winter
Kids wear coats and jackets.
Winter
Cold and cool rainy days going by.
Winter
Snow falling,
Winter
Children in school, learning each day.
Learning new things every new day,
Winter.
Then they come outside and play,
Winter.

Skylee Lyons
Age: 8

THANKSGIVING

T is for turkey that you can eat.
H is for the holiday time.
A is for the apple pie.
N is for the nice families.
K is for the kind people.
S is for the stuffing in turkey.
G is for giving.
I is for the important family.
V is for the very nice families.
I is for the Indians from the past.
N is for the nice people.
G is for the family gathering for Thanksgiving.

Robert Rosenbalm
Age: 9

THE GIANT TRAGEDY OF SEPTEMBER 11, 2001

Exactly one month after
They are still trying to clean up the disaster
for all the missing parts
has broken many hearts
for thousands of people died
and some are trying to hide
but there I lied
in my bed
because my head
was in pain
and the person who did it must be in shame
a war has happened
it might be the end
exactly one month after
from the big disaster
only a war has happened
but it is still a big deal

In memory of September 11, 2001

Amy McCue
Age: 12

A DAY I'LL NEVER FORGET

It's a day to save, to not forget.
It's a day to let our feelings consume us.
On September 11th, 2001,
a terrorists' siege, not since 1991.
The Pentagon went down,
with the Trade Center's Tower,
From a terrorists' attack, now it's all black.
It's a somber day for us all, some big, some small;
Many kids with no parents because of it all.
George Bush, snatch this while you can.
Take advantage of it, and prove to the United States
that you are the man who will give a helping hand,
to make peace, in the land.
You are the man that protects us all,
from some great, and some small.
Just think of all that perished.
Don't start a war,
those people are just like you and me.
It would dent the world's history;
Mr. Bush, this is the day, I will never forget.

Aimee Glenn
Age: 9

THANKSGIVING

T is for the turkey that is covered in gravy
H is for hot cocoa with melted marshmallows
A is for anything that I want to eat
N is for nodding my head yes or no
K is for knocking on each door
S is for snacking on pies
G is for goners who ate too fast
I is for invitations for Thanksgiving
V is for volunteering to do grace
I is for getting my food individually
N is for no school on Thanksgiving
G is for gobbling all of the food down

Miranda Ellis
Age: 9

T hankful for food
H arvest
A nd my mom and dad love it
N ovember... very cold
K ind to all the people
S tuffing all around
G ood food
I ndians
V arieties of food
"I 'm in the house eating"!
N ow holidays are best of all
G ood turkey, for a Thanksgiving dinner

Jessica Quillen
Age: 9

150

GOLDEN SUNSET

As you watch it with your wondering eyes,
The fish that looks like a golden sunset
It's the most beautiful thing you've ever seen.
You can talk to it, and it won't give you its opinion.
You can watch it and it will never stop.
As it swims around like a lightning bolt,
Darting from here to there, and corner to corner.
When you see bubbles coming from the fish
Just think of a few clouds floating in the sunset.
When it's in the fishbowl,
With your great imagination
Think of the bowl as the universe,
And the rising sun shining its beautiful glory.
As you watch the quiet sunset, just think...
You can watch the sunset all your life.

Christopher Van Cleave
Age: 10

SANTA'S REINDEER

These are the reindeers that live with Santa
One is Rudolph who came from Atlanta
Second is Dasher married to Sue
Third is Dancer sick with the flu
Next comes Prancer mighty and macho
Then we have Vixen who likes to eat nachos
Sixth is Comet as fast as a Concorde
Seventh is Cupid who drives a big Ford
Eighth is Donner who seems kind of crazy
The last one is Blitzen who is very lazy
I feel sorry for Santa
And his heavy sleigh
Who flies over the world on Christmas Day

Daniel Kiser
Age: 10

F amilies
E xcellent food
A loving holiday
S tuffing the turkey
T hankful

Evan Obrist
Age: 10

THE FOUR SEASONS

Winter, spring, summer, fall
These are the seasons
Four seasons and that is all
Winter is the coldest,
and most of all the boldest.
Spring is the time,
for the flowers to mime.
Summer's always hot,
the people sweat a lot.
Fall is for leaves,
to drop to their eaves.
These are the seasons
They are there for reasons
No more no less.

Michelle M. Smith
Age: 10

F ootball
E at turkey all day
A mericans
S tuffing
T hanksgiving

Brandon Goldblatt

RED, WHITE AND BLUE

Red, white and blue
We're just the same as you
I heard it on TV
I hear on the news
It made me mad it made me sad
Buildings went down
Many people died
Crying and sighing
Saying well we used to have the tallest
Buildings in the world
But now they are down
Red, white and blue
We're just the same as you

Shelley Leddon
Age: 10

Lifeless,
My dad sitting on the
Ground with tears in his
Eyes.

Lifeless, my
Dog lying on the bed, no
Life in his big brown puppy
Eyes.

Lifeless,
His bright, white fur wet and
Muddy with the black streak
Of a bike tire.

Lifeless,
Hate filled my heart when I
Heard the name Joe.

Alive,
As my little dog Pepe
Lifted his head to lick
My dad's face,
Alive!!!

Erica K. Dowden
Age: 11

Tyler
A friend
Plays dodge ball and flies up
Always likes to play what I play
Fun

Berkley Nilles
Age: 9

SKITTLES

Skittles Skittles, they taste so great,
Skittles Skittles, they even have grape,
Skittles Skittles, some are very berry,
Skittles Skittles, they even have cherry,
Skittles Skittles, some are sour,
Skittles Skittles, a candy to devour,
Skittles Skittles, some are tropical,
Skittles Skittles, they are classical,
Skittles Skittles, some are original,
Skittles Skittles, they're individual,
Skittles Skittles, they're all mine,
Skittles Skittles, they even have lime,
Skittles Skittles, up the wall,
Skittles Skittles, for one and all.

Lars Blazina
Age: 11

WHAT WAS THAT!

Crick,
Crack
What was that?
Was it a big fat cat?
Or a mouse that sat?
What
About
A
Stinky
Old bat?

What was it?
Was it Mr. Wendt knocking at my door?
Or perhaps a crack on the floor?
Or was it something more!

Kelly MacWhorter
Age: 10

Apple
warm, yummy
eating, baking, slicing
I love apple pie
Pie

Erin McCann
Age: 9

LINEMAN OF THE GAME

I got ready in my stance,
the sweat dripping down my face.
I could feel and see the fear they had for us.
The crowd was cheering.
I was lineman of the game.

The quarterback is ready he tenses up,
"Down!" he yells.
I can hear my stomach growling,
hungry for the tackle, RRRRRR!
The QB says "GO!"
I rip through the line aiming for my target the QB,
like an arrow piercing the air.
I was lineman of the game.

I hit him like a cannonball buzzing through the air,
ZZZZZZZZ,
then a clash and explosions erupt,
BOOOOOOOOOM!
He falls to the ground with a crash.
I jump up roaring with a booming blast!
I can hear Miles cheering, "OGRE!"
I yell like a crazed beast! ARGGGGHH!
I was lineman of the game.

I get into the huddle and hear the play.
The QB says, "GO!"
I hit the linemen with a crash!

CRACK! BANG! POW!
I try to get the QB but then I see the true target,
a running back!
I ran! I treaded the terrain like a tank.
Then like a bullet, "BOOM!"
I exploded and saved the tackle!
I was lineman of the game.

Richard C. Ogle
Age: 14

SPOT

I have a cat, his name is Spot.
He really likes to meow a lot.
He always sleeps on my mom's clean
clothes. All our whites turn black,
From all the hair on his back,
My mom says she's had it,
Then kicks him out.
The poor little lad.

Tomas Moriarty

MOUNTAINS

Mountains have snow,
Mountains have trees.
Mountains have snowboarders
And skiers.
Mountains are big,
Mountains have beautiful landscapes,
Mountains have log cabins.
Let's face it!
Mountains are beautiful.

Robby Schultz
Age: 8

My birdie, cute, friendly, funny,
lovable, obnoxious, weird, and determined.
And all of these, my bird is.

Tony DePellegrini

Blue is the bay on a summer's day.
  A cloudy sky is a silvery gray.
Mean purple waves crash sky-high.
  Tall green trees reach the sky.
White is the sea foam and the sea air.
  Gray are the beautiful mountains up there.
Orange is the sunset setting in the west.
  What colors do you like best?

Karina Robertson
Age: 11

It will soon be cold
Winter is beginning now
Snow will soon come down

Kevin Carroll

Flags
Flowing in the air
Plays with the wild wind
Red white blue
I love U

Carrina Clauson

There was a dog named Pete.
And he loved to eat meat.
He had a friend who was a man.
And cooked his meat in a pan.

Jill Morris
Age: 9

F rog that catches a fly.
O wl that lives in the tree.
R abbit that digs underground.
E agle that soars across the sky.
S quirrel that climbs up the tree.
T urtle that swims all around.

Zachary M. Teeny

T hankful
U nlucky turkey
R oasting turkey
K ind
E ating
Y um

Haleigh Novak
Age: 9

M aple tree
A pple pie
Y ummy dinner
F ootball
L oving family
O n Thanksgiving is a day when family gets together
W hen Thanksgiving comes so much food
E xciting holiday
R ainbows are good when Thanksgiving comes

Amber Cody
Age: 9

T hanksgiving
U se stuffing for your supper
R oasting meat
K indness
E xciting memories
Y ummy super

Ashley Perkins

I am a little witch!

I am a cute little witch
I fly around on my broom
I am a nice little witch
I fly on my broom on Halloween night
I go trick-or-treating on Halloween

I am a little witch!

Maria Kirby
Age: 9

N ice and flavorful,
I ce for
C old drinks,
K etchup on my burger.

K itchen chefs,
U nstoppable cooking,
L uscious food,
A nd all for me!
N umbing cold,
I ce cream in my mouth!

Nicholas M. Kulani
Age: 9

THANKSGIVING

Thanksgiving is a time to share,
Thanksgiving is a time to care,
Thanksgiving is not a time to hate,
With turkey dinners on our plates.
Thanksgiving is a time for family to gather 'round,
With a smile instead of a frown.
Thanksgiving

Cole Soderburg
Age: 9

Apples
sweet, crunchy
growing, sprouting, falling
food for my health
Fruit

Victoria Syhalath
Age: 9

THANKSGIVING

Thanksgiving is fun for family,
Friends and everyone.
It's a time for sharing and a time for caring.
We eat together no matter what the weather.
Thanksgiving

Melissa R. White
Age: 9

T hanksgiving
H arvest
A pple pie
N atives
K indness
F east
U nsolved tastes
L ove

Kawailehua Medeiros
Age: 9

THE AMERICAN FLAG

Flags, flags, flags.
You probably already knew,
That the colors of the American flag,
Are red, white, and blue.
Flying through the air in war or in peace.
Throughout night and throughout day,
It flies high, it flies proud.
Representing freedom all the way.

Jacquelyn A. Crews
Age: 10

WINTER

Winter is fun
With snow falling from the sky!
The weather is frosty.

Winter is snowball time.
Winter is when snow melts.
Then it is all over.

Sy Hoff
Age: 8

PRECIOUS BABY

Baby, baby, precious baby,
Born on Christmas Day.
No more room for him inside the inn,
Make his bed of hay.
Mama, Daddy, safe in the stable,
While the animals play,
The angels say to everyone,
"The star will lead the way."

Taylor N. Thompson
Age: 9

RAIN

Have you ever thought about the rain?
Sometimes I think it's a pain.
But the tippety-tap, the rippety-rap,
I think I'll be able to sustain.

Iean G. Drew
Age: 9

DRAGONFLY

Dragonfly, dragonfly, beast of the sky,
Blue like a beam, red like fire.
Dragonfly, dragonfly, beast of the sky,
Fluttering like a beautiful bee,
Flying in the bright blue sky,
Dragonfly, dragonfly, beast of the sky!

Travis D. Lowell
Age: 10

S ummer breezes,
E vening calm,
A utumn's dryness,
S omething that always comes and goes.
O vercast winter,
N othing less than blowing leaves,
S pring blossoms.

Dylan McNeill
Age: 9

B is for baseball
A is for amazing players
S is for several runs
E is for ERA that a pitcher has
B is for base hit
A is for America's favorite sport
L is for loving baseball
L is for left-handed pitchers

Reuben Smith
Age: 10

HALLOWEEN

H alloween is the time you get lots of candy.
A t night is when you go trick-or-treating.
L ights and music pop on when you step on the porches.
L iquid pours out of fake vampires' mouths.
O ver the hills are the jackpot houses of candy.
W icked witches walk around and they almost look real.
E verybody is dressed up on Halloween.
E verything is wicked and nerve-breaking.
N ever skip Halloween, it's almost every kid's life.

Lindsey Racheal Gard
Age: 10

Cake, cake, cake it tastes so great
I would love to have a pool-sized cake
It tastes like gushy chocolate squeezing
Through my teeth cake, cake, cake
It does taste great!

Matthew Todhunter
Age: 11

RAIN

droplets of rain fall from the sky
dark black clouds perform a dance
soon the lightning hits with a flash
but you are safe and sound inside

Amanda Mielke
Age: 11